Puppetry
With & Without Ventriloquism

Written by Lynne Edwards

Published by Groovy Teaching
Mount Martha, Victoria, Australia
groovyteaching.com.au

Copyright ©2022 Lynne Edwards

Cover and illustrations by Lynne Groovy
Edwards
ISBN: 978-0-6454847-2-4
First Edition

Table of Contents

Chapter One

Why become a puppeteer?

There is something truly magical about the innocent delight children have when they have quality interaction with puppets that they believe are 'alive'. They can become so totally immersed in the puppet's world that they don't even question the reality of it all. The joy that can result from a confident puppeteer bringing to life an adorable puppet is a wonderful thing.

In the many years I have been using puppets in my classroom, I have found them to be an invaluable tool in breaking down barriers. Young students will do anything for the reward of 'puppet time' at the end of the day. Puppets are a great reward, but also wonderful class mood 'pick me ups', brain breaks, self esteem boosters and all round entertainers.

Children see puppets as 'safe non judgemental' friends. It has been truly heartwarming to see the delight in children who might rarely smile, who have been through difficult circumstances, or who have low self esteem. Puppets can have a very positive effect in so many ways. If you are a budding comedian, puppets can also bring joy and laughter to teens and adults!

This book gives some basic advice for new puppeteers whether young or old, a teacher, youth leader or a child interested in becoming a puppeteer. If you have never attempted puppetry, don't be afraid to give it a try. Often the fear of being a 'bad ventriloquist' and not being 'good enough' to capture the children's imaginations, prevents people from taking the puppet plunge. The fear

Some of my puppet family. Milton at the top, my very first puppet. Underneath Milton, from left to right are Hank the bear, Greg the Orangutan and Hannah (Milton's little sister).

of your audience not believing the illusion of reality and mocking your puppeteering attempts can be too strong a deterrent for people to give it a go.

Believe me, you can do this, and you don't even need to use ventriloquism if you don't want to. There are other ways to have puppets 'communicate' with the audience. One of these ways is the 'Whisper' method which I will describe in detail in Chapter 3.

I am so glad I decided to buy a puppet early in my teaching career. That puppet, Milton, and the puppet family I have grown since then, have brought much joy to my students and I over the years. They have brought laughter and happiness to many tiring school days. They have provided a creative outlet for children who decide to become puppeteers themselves, whether with expensive puppets or even socks! I admit they have also been one of the best 'bribes' in encouraging good behaviour with the promise of a puppet session as a reward. They are such a wonderful tool for injecting some positive energy into your day.

I'm not suggesting it is always easy to start though. I was teaching 9 year olds when I first began teaching and decided to introduce a puppet to my teaching tool box. I initially tried ventriloquism, but was so unconvincing I nearly gave up on puppeteering altogether. The students rolled their eyes at my poor attempts at hiding my mouth movements. I tried using a believable puppet voice but wasn't consistent and it just didn't fool the savvy youngsters at all. They didn't engage at all well with the puppet routines I was offering either and the attempts at humour fell flat. I nearly gave up at this point but am very glad that I persisted.

My very first puppet, Milton and I. In 30 years of being my school puppet, Milton has been loved by at least 15000 students. I'm fairly sure he will be more entrenched in their memory than myself and I think that's awesome!

Audience criticism can knock your confidence and motivation. Money was tight for me at the time I bought Milton, my first puppet. I bought the puppet from a company in the US. It was shipped to Australia and cost qa lot of money, so I really wanted to make it worthwhile.

This cost motivated me to keep trying and not give up. It made me determined to find ways to make it work. When there was no internet and very little written information to help me out, I had to rely on books and watching live puppeteers. Now there are Youtube videos with skilled ventriloquists young and old with advice. I highly recommend you spend time perusing these resources, but also hope I will be able to shortcut your puppeteering learning with insights from my personal experience. Also there is little information on puppeteering without ventriloquism, which I cover in this book.

In deciding to persevere I wanted to find a way for the puppet to communicate, without me doing 'the voice' and with an explanation as to why it couldn't talk itself. In the coming chapters I will describe the method I used and have refined over the years. Believe me, it works and makes puppeteering a whole lot easier! First though, it's very important to find a puppet to work with, and in the next Chapter I will explain the importance of choosing the right puppet and what to look for.

I am so glad I decided to buy a puppet and persevere with it! What a wonderful asset to my teaching these puppets have been. I believe that every primary elementary/nursery/kindergarten teacher would have more positive and enriched classrooms if they incorporated puppets as a regular part of their teaching program.

Chapter Two
Choosing your first puppet.

It is very important to choose your first puppet wisely. You can practise using sock puppets and hand puppets, or borrowing puppets, but when it comes to a puppet you want to perform with, take your time to find one that really appeals to you.

Can you imagine an interesting personality when you look at the puppet? Do you like the look and feel of it? Does it have an expression that is interesting and can show a variety of emotions? Is it a good size for you to hold? Does it have rods or do you insert your hands inside a mitt? Is it within your price range?

All these factors are very important. Good puppeteers will actually become very fond of their puppets and develop their personalities to the point where they are like friends. I love all of my puppets and they have become like an extension of my family.

When shopping for your puppet, don't think of it as a toy, think of it as a little character you are adopting and will cherish. I remember seeing a photo of my first puppet 'Milton', and immediately finding him endearing. His little face with the big black glasses immediately had me formulating a potential personality in my mind. He was more expensive than I had planned for, and I had to have him posted from the USA to Australia, but the heart wants what the heart wants!

Spending that extra money and having to wait for his arrival, made the whole thing more special in the end and I was more careful to look after and treasure him.

That was in 1993 and he's been loved by myself and thousands of children over the years ever since. I'm so glad I made that decision.

I suggest you also buy a box of some kind to keep the puppet in. I like to buy old suitcases or chests from opportunity shops. This adds an air of mystery and an element of a magical 'reveal' as you carefully remove the puppet from the case, talking to them as if they are real as you position your hand.

Also children these days won't often see old cases, once again adding a 'special' element to the whole experience.

Take your time and find a special puppet that you will enjoy working with and bringing to life. I highly recommend you find and visit a physical shop that sells a variety of puppets. I was lucky purchasing my first puppet without 'trying him on' first. Since then however I have always tried puppets out before buying one.

A puppet might look appealing and I have that instant connection with their potential character, however the physical movement aspect might not work. For example the head might be difficult to move sideways or on an angle. The mouth might be difficult to open or not very expressive. The interior foam might be flimsy and likely to fall apart quickly with regular use. Also the size can be deceiving in online photos.

Wide/hard mouthed puppets

I like my puppets to be taller than 30". Children older than 6 are able to work with these larger puppets too, although starting them off with smaller less expensive puppets is probably a good idea in case they lose interest.

When you place a puppet on your arm and turn it's head to look at you, does it make you smile? That's awesome and might just be the time you say "Welcome to my family."

Hank the bear sitting on two off the old suitcases my puppets 'live' in. I place the pictures and letters my students make for the puppets in the cases too.

Chapter Three

The Whisper Method.

The 'Whisper Method' I believe is the perfect way to begin your puppeteering journey. Instead of using ventriloquism to give your puppet a voice (which can be very risky if you can't do it well), you have the puppet whisper into your ear, and then you tell the children what the puppet said. This might sound really simple, but to be done well, you need to take into account the following suggestions.

Ideally, with very young children as the audience, you want the puppet to be seen as a real life little puppet person/animal. You must have a back story as to why you are the only one who can hear the puppet. Remember that children are likely to have seen people using hand puppets for fun, taking them on and off, leaving them lying around etc. They know they're not real. You need to do something different to make your puppet seem uniquely alive. I cover this in the next Chapter and give you the backstory that I use which you can use as is, or modify to suit yourself.

You need to differentiate your puppet from all the other toy puppets the children will encounter. Why is it that your puppet can move itself and 'talk' to you, when other puppets don't do anything? The children can see your hands in and/or on the puppet, so you need to have an explanation as to why it isn't just you controlling the puppet (even though you actually are!).

You need to be prepared to answer the following questions and statements from children:

- "It's not real, you're doing it."
- "You have your hand in it"
- "It's not a real life puppet."
- "There's no such thing as a real life puppet."
- "My parents say your puppet isn't real."
- "Why can't we hear it talk?"
- "Why can't it talk in my ear?"
- "Why are you the only one that can make it come to life?"

It's important that you respect the children's opinions and encourage their questions without losing the magic you are trying to create. Let me share some of my 'go to' answers for all of these questions for you to use/adapt for yourself.
I say things like this:

- "I understand that you don't believe in it, that's ok, but I do."
- Yes I have my hands in/on the puppet, but it's using my energy to move itself. The puppet is moving my hand, isn't that clever!
- It is a real life puppet, I know that because it's moving me, I'm not moving it! I can also hear what it tells me AND it came from a real life puppet factory (I'll explain this in the next chapter)
- If your parents don't believe, that's ok, everyone can have their own opinion including you, I don't mind. I just know what I believe!

- You can't hear it talk because only the puppet's master can hear it and make it move (more on this in the next chapter)

It's important you are ready to answer these questions with conviction. I think it's also important not to be too insistent about them believing you. Allowing them to believe or not believe is perfectly fine and actually is a respectful approach. Let's face it, we are telling fibs, so there's no need to go overboard. If you're not into telling fibs to children then you can admit you're a storyteller and your puppet is one of your characters. I like to keep the magic alive though. Then again I've also been known to dress as the Easter bunny!

In Chapter 6 I give you some more of the answers that I use for some difficult questions I frequently encounter. Using the whisper method and the associated backstory described in the next chapter, the children learn that you are the special owner of the puppet and the only one able to help it communicate and move. You will need to practise manipulating the puppet so it looks like it is whispering to you, opening and closing it's mouth near your ear realistically.
Practise moving the puppets mouth near your ear and then back to the 'looking at you' position (as if waiting for your answer) quickly. When the puppet is 'whispering' you need to be opening and closing its mouth for about the amount of time it would take to say what you are going to relay to the audience.

The puppet should always move naturally, looking around and fidgeting even when you're not looking at it. It can pull faces and do funny things seemingly on its own (while you are engaged in a conversation with someone for example). All of this enables conversation and physical interactions between you, the audience and the puppet without the need for ventriloquism.

The beauty of this method is that anyone can do it and there is no need for making up a voice or attempting ventriloquism. Children love this just as much and using the back story detailed in the next chapter, you can explain why only you can hear what the puppet says. It's easy, it works and you can do it confidently with minimum practise.

Hank
'Whispering'
to me.

Chapter Four
The Back Story:
Explaining the puppet's life.

I cannot stress enough the importance of first explaining to the students how you came to find a 'real life' puppet before you introduce them to it. I tell the story of the 'magical puppet factory on the other side of the world' which I have refined over my years of teaching and puppeteering.

You are welcome to use it as it is, modify it for yourself, or come up with your own original story. It is very important to be invested in the story as you are telling it. Be enthusiastic and share your apparent excitement and gratitude that you are so lucky to have this magical puppet. The more elaborate the story and expressiveness in the story telling, the more the children will believe it and be enthralled by it. My story is this:

When I was a child I went on a holiday overseas with my family. We were trekking through a forest on the other side of the world. It was a really remote place, my parents loved adventure. We often visited far away countries. Once we were in this remote place when suddenly we stumbled across a beautiful but unusual house. It was colourful and large, more like a castle. There was a sign outside that said "Phoebe Buckle's Puppet Factory".

It was really weird to see a factory in a place like this. We wondered if it really was a puppet factory and decided to investigate.

My parents knocked on the door and an old woman with a kind face appeared. She introduced herself as Phoebe Buckle. We told her that we were from Australia and were travelling the world. We expressed our surprise to see a house and factory in the middle of a forest. Phoebe laughed and and asked us if we'd like to come in and see her puppets. I was so excited. "Of course" we said, and she took us to the back of her house where there was a huge triangular room filled with puppets of all shapes and sizes as well as sewing machines, rolls of material and stacks of timber.There were small puppets on one wall of the room, large puppets on another wall, and shelves with suitcases on the third wall. I asked what was in the suitcases and Phoebe said they were her very special puppets and she doesn't often show those ones to people. She explained that the small puppets were simple hand puppets for children. She said the bigger puppets had rods to help humans move their arms, and they were suitable for children and adults to use.With a twinkle in her eye she said that the puppets in the suitcases were just like the big puppets, but had one major difference. She put her hands on my shoulders and put her face close to mine. She whispered, "Can you keep a secret?" I nodded, held out my little finger and said "Yes". She then said "Do you pinky promise?"She held out her crooked little finger and I held out mine and said "Yes I pinky promise!" We linked pinky fingers and she led me over to the shelf of suitcases.

A visual interpretation of what Phoebe's Magical Puppet Factory in the forest might look like.

Phoebe took an old suitcase from the shelf, opened it and took out a lovely girl puppet with long red hair. "This is Matilda" she said. The puppet looked at me and then seemed to whisper something in Phoebe's ear. Phoebe relayed the message: "Matilda said she really likes your polkadot shirt." The puppet was looking at me and I had this really strange feeling that the puppet was REALLY looking at me......like it was ALIVE! Phoebe saw the expression on my face and said "I know what you're thinking, and you're right, she's a real life puppet and she's alive."

I couldn't believe it. I was in a magical house in the forest where there were real life puppets! I'm sure you can imagine how excited we were! At first we didn't believe Phoebe that the puppet was real, but after a while it was obvious that Matilda had her own personality and was in control of her movements. We had no idea real life puppets existed and my parents had so many questions.

Phoebe and her puppet, Matilda, chatted with us all day and told us about the magic of this part of the forest. Phoebe had built her house there because she wanted to make her puppets in a quiet beautiful place. What she didn't know is that every now and then when she made a puppet, and when she put her hand in it for the first time, it would come alive. Phoebe said the first time it happen she was frightened, but it didn't take long for her to realise that the real life puppets were harmless, curious, funny and loveable friends.

She never knows which ones will come alive and it doesn't happen very often.

Phoebe explained that when your hand is inside them, they draw on your human energy and make your hand move the way they want. When you hold the rods attached to their hands, they use the human energy that flows through the metal in the rods to move your hands. So your hands are moving the puppet, but the puppets are moving your hands….amazing right! Phoebe also told us that the first human to hold a real life puppet, becomes that puppet's 'Master' for life. The puppet can only use that particular human's energy and can only talk to that human. Nobody else will be able to hear what they are saying, or help them to move. Being a puppet's master is a very big responsibility and a very special gift.

We had such an amazing day and when it was time to go, Phoebe said to me: "You are such a lovely girl and I trust you can keep a secret and not tell anyone where my magic factory is. I would like to give you a gift." She then pulled down an old striped grey suitcase and said "The case might look plain but what's inside certainly isn't. He's a real life puppet named Milton and he has real life magic. I only finished making him yesterday and haven't put my hand inside his body yet but I'm sure he's real, because I can feel the magic around him. If you hold him properly first, he will be yours forever. It's a big responsibility and you must never ever give him away. He won't work for anyone else and will be miserable if he's left alone, or with other humans for long periods of time and can't come alive very often."

Can you imagine how excited I was! My parents couldn't believe it either. They promised they would help me look after the puppet. They thanked Phoebe so much and watched as she pulled Milton out of the case and handed him to me. I loved Milton from the moment I saw him, and when I put my hand in him for the first time, he moved all by himself. It was such a strange feeling having something else moving my body!

Phoebe said she thinks it is just some strange kind of magic that exists in that particular place that gives life to her puppets sometimes. She said that perhaps it's like a fairy kind of magic, as she's seen fairies occasionally near toadstools among the trees. Even that's amazing isn't it, because I've never seen a fairy!

Phoebe told us that the puppets only can talk and move by themselves when their human owner is holding them. They like to be in a dark safe place and go to sleep when they are not with their human, which is why she puts them in suitcases. The puppets use the humans energy to move.

Milton leaned over and whispered in my ear "Hello I'm Milton and I am your best friend." I could hear him! He had this soft little voice and I asked my parents "Can you hear that?" but they couldn't hear anything. It was magic. I had never been so happy.

I have looked after Milton ever since. When I became a teacher I was excited to show him to my students. I have introduced him to thousands of school children and everyone loves him.

He can be a bit naughty sometimes, but he's also very caring. It's really important that I'm the only one that holds him, but through me he can talk to anyone and he loves having chats
with children. He's amazing and I love him."

This is the story I tell my students. The more detail you give, the more believable it is. You can embellish the details as you tell the story. The important thing is that it explains why nobody else can use the puppet and feel it move by itself, or hear the puppet talk. It explains why the children see you moving the puppet with your hands, but the puppet is actually moving itself. It explains why the puppets are kept in a case (which is important in a classroom situation where it protects your puppet from being handled a lot and wearing out. I never let students handle my 'real life' puppets. It helps maintain the realism of the story. I do choose one student each time the puppet is out, to cuddle the puppet. They love this.

Have fun telling the story, there is nothing quite as lovely as seeing the innocent excitement of young children believing that sweet harmless magic exists in the world, and they can actually be a part of it.

Chapter Five
Puppet Manipulation

Once you've chosen a puppet and found a case for it, the next step is to practise manipulating the puppet so that it looks life-like. It is important that you get into the habit of always giving the puppet life whenever you are holding it. Even if you are on your own, or you are talking to someone about something unrelated to the puppet, always have it looking around, looking at you, moving it's hand, scratching its nose etc. Even when I am on my own, my puppets are 'alive' if they are attached. It's become a habit and it really is important. For example, if I am using the puppet in a class and another teacher comes in to ask me something, the puppet will be looking around, or nodding while I'm talking. The children see this and it makes it even more believable. If it wasn't alive it would just be limp right? Things you can have it do when you are not directly communicating with it are:

- looking around
- pulling faces at others in the room
- waving
- scratching itself
- touching your face (then you say "hey don't, can't you see I'm talking?")
- tickling you or someone else,
- playing peek a boo
- picking it's nose (then you notice and ask it to stop)

Some puppets have big hands that are basically like gloves you put your own hand in. I do have a puppet like this, but it's not my preference. Firstly the hands are very big in relation to the size of the puppet which looks a little odd. Secondly you need one hand for the head, so only one hand can be used, leaving the other puppet hand looking limp and lifeless. I say to the children that I wish I had 3 hands so the puppet could use it's other hand, but like I said before, it's not my preference. I much prefer to use rods on a puppet's hands. One on each hand, both manipulated by my non dominant hand. This takes practise and I suggest you start with one rod first. You need to be able to move it in all directions and reach most parts of the puppets body and yours (so it can touch your face and tickle you etc. Once you have practised with one rod, start introducing the second. It's actually not as difficult as it looks. I have one rod between my pointer and middle finger and the other rod between my middle and ring finger. You need to find the hand and rod position that suits you. Try to move each hand independently first. Once you can do simple independent movements, try clapping the hands together. This will take practise and you can always place one of the hands on the puppets lap and clap the other onto it, which is easier. Other movements to practise are:

- Hi-5
- Shrugging
- Patting chin in a thinking pose (great for those moments you need a little extra time to come up with a response!)
- Pointing at objects

- Clapping high and low
- Rubbing hands together
- Dancing (waving arms in the air etc)
- Putting hands to cheeks for a 'surprise' look
- Tickling itself and you
- Scratching
- Playing with its hair or yours.

Once you get used to using the rods, it's amazing how you can manipulate the puppets to do just about anything! It's ok for the audience to know there are rods and see your hands moving. Remember you tell them that the puppet is actually using your energy and controlling your hands!

Along with hand gestures, you also need to be able to move your puppets mouth and tilt its head in ways that express different emotions. A puppet with a soft mouth enables you to change the shape of the mouth which makes expressions easier to show. A puppet with a hard mouth requires you to rely on head tilts, movements and hand gestures to give a variety of expressions. This is not to say you should look for a soft mouthed puppet, as in my experience they can be more fragile long term and can get 'out of shape' more easily with lots of use. I have a little family of 'real life' puppets now and the soft mouth ones (Milton, Hank and Hanna) I don't use as often in order to preserve them, but I do enjoy using them a lot, as they can pull some very funny faces which the children love. As with anything, practise makes perfect. Whilst learning you can always complain to the children that the puppet is trying to move your hands too much and your fingers aren't used to moving like that!

Young children enjoying manipulating full sized puppets!

Chapter Six
Conversation Plans and Performance Ideas

When introducing your puppet to an audience, it's a very good idea to have a conversation plan in your mind. This is just a framework that the conversation between the puppet and your audience can be directed within. It might be just one main idea you are going to talk about, and you 'wing it' after that. It might be a detailed plan with more than one subject to be covered. I've been doing it for a long time and I still think of one thing to get a conversation started. This might be a joke the puppet wants to tell for example. After that I can facilitate a question/answer session, or the children can tell the puppet things (maybe it was their birthday or something like that).

If you don't find impromptu chatter easy, you don't want to be sitting there with nothing to say, so be prepared and have some sort of a plan. The following are some simple framework examples you can use and modify for you and your puppet.

Naughty Puppet Example Plan

1. Puppet whispers he doesn't like one of the audience's clothes
2. You say it's not very nice and give reasons why we should be kind
3. Puppet then says something about your clothes.
4. You tell the puppet that if he's not kind he won't be going to the zoo with you next weekend.
5. Puppet gets sad about that and starts to say nice things to everyone, but some are a bit strange like "I really like your front tooth."
6. Ask the children if they have any suggestions for when you take your puppet to the zoo. What animals should he look for etc.
7. Puppet says you look like a monkey. You pretend to be fed up and say "That's it, no zoo."
8. Puppet is really sad and sorry and promises to be good. You say "Are you sure you're going to be good?" Puppet nods. You then look to the children and say "Oh that's good, I'm glad." While you are looking away from the puppet he shakes his head. Look back at him and have him nodding. Look away and have him shaking. The children will start yelling at you that the puppet is lying. Keep it going for a while and then pretend to catch the puppet out. This is a favourite routine of mine that children love and you can repeat in many different scenarios.

Add your own lines and adlib along the way to make the plan personal and responsive to your audience reactions.

The plan in a nutshell:

- Intro
- Clothing insult 1
- Kindness lecture
- Clothing insult 2
- Zoo bribe
- Fake niceness
- Zoo suggestions from audience
- Monkey insult
- Yes No deception.

Greg is a very cheeky and active monkey.

Shy Puppet
Example Plan

1. Introduce puppet
2. Puppet snuggles up to you, hiding face. You explain that they're a bit shy.
3. Coax the puppet into having a peep at the children and instruct the children to smile sweetly to give the puppet confidence.
4. Puppet looks up gradually and gives a shy wave. Ask the children to wave back.
5. Puppet whispers to you asking the children how old they are. Then the puppet tells them how old it is in puppet years and human years. You can then explain what this means. (Puppets are made a certain age and are that forever. That is their puppet age. Their human age is how long it is since they were made).
6. Puppet asks if anyone would like to hear a riddle. Then she changes her mind and says she's scared nobody will laugh (this is where you say to the children that they need to laugh to make her feel better). Then she tells a simple riddle such as: I have a tail and a head but no body, what am I? (a coin), children guess, laugh etc.
7. Ask the children if they know any riddles. Have the puppet guess some ridiculous answers for fun.

The plan in a nutshell:
- Intro
- Peep
- Wave
- Interact
- Riddle
- Audience questions and riddles, puppet responds.

These 2 examples of conversation plans give you a basis for conversation between you and the audience. Most of the time you will go off on tangents as the audience interacts, which is wonderful.
I strongly suggest you always have a bit of a plan/idea in your mind of how to get some conversation going and engage the audience from the start. I like to have a couple of simple riddle or jokes up my sleeve that my puppet can tell the children if there's a lull in the conversation/performance. Then you can ask the audience if they have a riddle to share too. That fills in a few minutes!

To finish performances, I usually have the puppet start to yawn and I tell the children it's getting tired and needs to go back in the case for a rest. You can also have the puppet start to fall asleep on your shoulder which is cute (put they're hands over their eyes, or have their face turned into your shoulder/neck.)

When you are beginning your puppeteering journey keep the sessions short. Tell the children that real life puppets get tired easily. As you become more confident you can increase the time. Be kind to yourself. You'll get there and it's worth it.

Chapter Seven
Answering difficult questions

Children can be smart and savvy so be prepared to answer their tricky questions. It's important to maintain your confidence and stick to your backstory. You need to look like no question fazes you because you know the truth (which is actually not the truth but it's fun!)
Here are some of my answers to tricky questions.

Question: Is it real?

Answer: It's a real life puppet, but it's not a person.

Question: Can it see and hear when you're not there?

Answer: Yes but it can't move. It's quite happy to go to sleep in the case and real life puppets can sleep happily for days.

Question: Can I buy one?

Answer: No you can only get them from the magic puppet factory and I promised to never reveal where that is.

Question: Why does it go in a case?

Answer: Because real life puppets don't feel safe outside without their special human owner. Imagine if someone else tried to use them. They could see and hear but not move. That would be a bit scary. (This explanation also prevents children from trying to take the puppet out themselves.

Question: Why doesn't it talk out loud?

Answer: I don't know why they can't, I only know that they can whisper to their human owner and only their human owner can hear them. It's amazing isn't it!

Question: Why does it have to be a secret where they come from?

Answer: Because if lots of people found out about these magic puppets they would all want one. Can you imagine thousands and thousands of people all going to the little factory in the forest harassing the poor owner? She was such a lovely old woman and she would never be able to make enough for everyone. Some people might try to steal them also because they are so special and everyone wants something magical!
We are just so lucky that we get to experience it and know the secret ourselves.

Question: Do they eat and drink?

Answer: They talk about it and say they have favourite foods, but in fact they can't really eat and drink because they don't have a stomach or any of the organs we have. I don't tell them that though because they might get upset, so I just go along with their food stories.

Question: Do they wear out or get broken?

Answer: Yes they are made of material and if we are not very careful and gentle, they will wear out quickly. If that happens they just have to stay in their case. It's lucky that they are always happy in their case. They can even stay in their case for weeks and they don't mind.

Question: Do they feel pain?

Answer: No they don't, which is why we can glue their eyes back on, and stitch them up if they start to come apart.

Question: My parents said your puppet isn't real.

Answer: Of course it's very difficult to believe in magic. That's ok. I know what I believe but you don't have to believe the same and neither do your parents. It's a good thing to accept people's different opinions on things. My puppet told me she doesn't mind if some people don't believe she's real, and I don't mind either.

Chapter Eight
Ventriloquism for the brave

Let's talk ventriloquism.

It's not easy at all to fool children, but it IS easy to have fun with ventriloquism without the embarrassment of being caught 'moving your lips'.

When I decided I'd like to try some ventriloquism it was after I had spent quite some time using the whisper method. This meant that I already was able to manipulate the puppet and could concentrate on 'doing the voice'. I recommend you do the same and become quite proficient in manipulation before adding the skill of ventriloquism to your puppeteering repertoire.

I bought a brand new puppet especially for my ventriloquism routines and told my students that I was going to learn ventriloquism with this new puppet that IS NOT a real life puppet. It was important that my attempts at ventriloquism didn't interfere with my established real life puppet stories. Therefore introducing a new puppet and clarifying that it wasn't a real life puppet was important. Then I told the students that I was going to use a different voice to my own and try to make it look like the puppet was talking and not me. I was going to try to not move my lips and hopefully the voice wouldn't sound too much like my own. I asked them to help me by giving me feedback on my performance.

Surprisingly, but pleasingly, what I found was that the students enjoyed seeing the puppet just as much when they knew I was doing the voice. They still responded and reacted to it when they knew it wasn't really talking itself. It took all the pressure off while I was improving my skill. It was a great way to learn without the worry. I highly recommend you do this and once you are confident you can progress to performing without explanation. The added teaching bonus is that the students could learn by example how to start doing ventriloquism themselves. I would get a little stuck trying to say words like 'probably.' So I would stop and laugh and admit to my difficulty. Then I would ask them to try to say the word themselves and help me out. Many of my students decided they wanted to get or make a puppet and do ventriloquism themselves as they had firsthand experience watching me learn.

Another thing I highly recommend is practising both in front of a mirror and walking around your house, having conversations with your puppet. It's important with ventriloquism that you get into the rhythm of 'puppet then you', and you don't accidentally speak in your own voice at the wrong time. This takes PRACTISE but it is amazing how suddenly it just clicks and becomes easy AND FUN! I do think it's helpful to have designated ventriloquism puppets. If I tried to do ventriloquism with puppets I usually use the whisper method with, I would automatically be putting them to my ear instead of opening their mouths. Just as you get used to adapting to each puppets personality, you can get used to each puppet's form of communication.

Now to the technical and more difficult aspect of ventriloquism which is the skill of talking without moving your lips. Next I will share the basic 'how to's' of ventriloquism, including those tricky letters that you usually cannot say without moving your lips.

Ventriloquism basics

So how do you talk without moving your lips? Some words are easy, but some are quite difficult. In this chapter I'll endeavour to clarify it for you.

The first thing to master is your mouth position.

Smile a little and have your lips slightly apart, but check in a mirror that your tongue can't be seen moving in your mouth. Having your top and bottom teeth touching, or almost touching helps a lot but you don't want to look like your grimacing. Find a position that is comfortable for you, hides your tongue, looks pleasant and is easy to change in and out of.

Once you have a position you are happy with, look in a mirror and practise saying the following easy sentences without moving your mouth position:

- I like to go to the zoo to see the rhinos and donkeys.
- You can see that I don't like dirt in the kitchen.
- Look at the strange child running outside in the rain.
- Let's go and see the stars in the sky tonight.
- Can you do the dishes in the sink
- I like to eat lollies.

It really isn't that difficult to say most letters and words without moving your lips. There are however some letters within words that are more challenging. These letters will require a fair amount of practise to conquer but using the methods I suggest, or experimenting with your own methods you will get there. It is not impossible!
The letters in the alphabet that are difficult to say without moving your lips are these:

B F M P V W

Everyone's mouth is unique, so something that works for one person might not work for another. So the following suggestions are just things that I've found work for me. Experiment with these suggestions but also don't hesitate to try other things.

To make a B sound, I instead say the letter D, but I put my tongue further forward in my mouth, closer to my front teeth to soften the sound. So to practise, say the letter B out loud, then try to replicate the sound with a soft D.

Try saying these sentences in front of a mirror. Then ask a friend or family member to watch you saying them to give you feedback on how well you are hiding your mouth movement. This is important, as our movements often change as we try to interact with others, rather than being able to focus purely on ourselves in a mirror.

- Brian likes to bury bones.
- Be your best self and be kind.
- Do you belong to a basketball club?
- I like blue bracelets and big bracelets.
- My bicycle is broken and is being fixed.

To make an F sound use the soft 'th' sound and once again put your tongue behind your teeth This works really well for most people. Practise saying 'feather' to train your brain to distinguish between the real 'th' sound and the pretend F. Then try saying these phrases:

- I wish I could fly to France.
- Frank has fifty freckles.
- I was frightened by Frankenstein.
- Freedom is a fantastic thing.
- Finally I found my lost phone.

Replace M with N but also use your tongue behind your teeth (not necessarily on them, but in your mouth)

- Please buy me a muffin.
- Maybe you could make more money?
- Mickey plays badminton.
- My mother is mad at me.
- Who put muddy marks on my mat?

Replace P with T putting your tongue on the back of your teeth and giving it a little flick as it releases.

- Pretty pearls are nice to put on.
- Can you eat prickly pears?
- Put on your pink pants.
- Place that plate on the table.
- Who put the pot plant on the picnic blanket?

Replace V with hard 'TH' sound. This one works really well and is relatively simple.

- Victor craves vanilla ice-cream.
- Have you been in the cave?
- I have various varieties of vegetables.
- That is a vivid shade of violet.
- He was a victim of vile behaviour.

Replace W with L but push it from the back of your throat. Or you can try simply saying W by breathing out as you say it.

- William was always working.
- When did you water the plants?
- Why did you wash the dog today?
- Where is the white wagon?
- I want a chewy waffle.

Once again, remember that these are only suggestions and you may find other ways that suit you better.

Once you are able to say these difficult letters on their own within words such as 'very' 'friend' and 'water', you can then try words with more than one challenging letter. This includes difficult words like probably, move, pram, from, and brave.

Practise your ventriloquism in front of a mirror and family/friends, but also I find it hugely beneficial to film myself. You can really see your progress watching yourself and you'll be quite surprised at how good you are after a short period of time. You may think you are moving your lips more than you actually are. Try to stay positive and give yourself credit where credit is due!

It takes time and practise to do ventriloquism well, which is why I suggest you let your audience of children know that you are learning, until such time as you are confident. Then you can use the same backstory that was used for the whisper method, and let the magic happen!

You can do it!

Chapter Nine
Adding to your puppet family

If you find you enjoy puppetry as much as I do, you might also from time to time add to your puppet family. Every puppet you choose should be carefully selected and you need to give each a very distinct personality. If you are doing ventriloquism they also need to have a distinct voice. Children will become suspicious if all your puppets have the same voice! I like to also give each puppet at least one distinctive characteristic, and one that is amusing. My puppet family consists of:

- Milton, who loves to flick his glasses off, and always asks the children to take him to McDonalds so I give him a lecture about healthy eating.

- Hannah, a little girl who always tries to suck her thumb when I'm not looking. She also likes to kick her shoes off.

- Archie, a young boy who is very shy and says he can move around by himself whenever I'm asleep. He makes up stories about driving my car and riding my dog.

- Hank, a bear that thinks he can tell the children's futures. He makes up all sorts of far fetched stories about them and gets really sad if they don't believe him, so I ask the children to pretend to believe. **44.**

- Greg, an orangutan that farts, never stops swinging, and loves going for rides on the children's heads.

- Barry, a male teacher that is always grumpy about the way the children look (messy hair etc) and is really old fashioned. He doesn't like technology and thinks children should work harder. He argues with them and drives them crazy with his old fashioned ideas. The children find it funny that I roll my eyes when he's not looking at me.

- Rosie, my main ventriloquist puppet who is a bit of a rebel and encourages cheekiness. She loves to sing but has a terrible singing voice which makes the children laugh. She also gets frightened easily and screams (when children sneeze etc).

Having more than one puppet character also helps to keep your routines fresh and interesting for you as well as the children. I do suggest you take your time though and don't try to practise with too many puppets at once. Develop each puppet's personalities over time until you feel you really know what they would say or do in any given situation. This makes it much easier when you allow the children to ask questions.

I have had each puppet for at least a year before I introduce a new one. It really does take time to develop and become comfortable with the puppet's personalities and be able to keep it consistent.

I do find it helps keep it interesting for me having multiple puppets with various personality traits.

You can have each puppet in its own case, or have one big chest for all of them. I tell my students they can draw pictures or write letters to the puppets and I put them in the case with the puppets. It's really adorable to see some of the treasures the puppets receive from their fans.

Rosie is a 'Pubbets' brand Australian made puppet.

Chapter Ten
Final Words:
You've got this!

In summary, the two easy methods I recommend are the Whisper Method and the Ventriloquism method using substitute letters and having the children 'in the know' to begin with. Don't be disheartened if you have some stumbles at first, always be prepared to laugh at yourself and carry on. Children are very forgiving as long as you seem relaxed and keep it amusing.

If you start ventriloquism with a puppet that you openly declare is 'not real life' and you are just using it to practise your ventriloquism skills, you really do relieve the pressure on yourself to perform perfectly. Also it is a great encouragement for students to try it themselves when they see 'how' to practise because of the example you have set.

The Whisper method is by far the easiest method to use. It works, the children believe it if you sell the backstory and never waiver in your conviction. You can use this method alone, as I did for years, or you can use both methods with different puppets. If you really love a challenge you can practise your ventriloquism and only use that method. Whichever method you use, be kind to yourself and don't worry too much about being 'amazing'.

Children love puppets so you have room to move with the expertise or otherwise of your performance quality. The most important thing is to try to stay relaxed, have fun and show that you love and care for your puppet like it is a little human.

I have been using puppets In my classrooms for over 30 years and can honestly say I have had hundreds of students visit me years later and say the puppets were one of their favourite things about school! Many students go on to buy their own puppets and use them in youth leadership roles, or even with their own children (yes I'm that old). This warms my heart and will warm yours too if you just give it a try. Don't take it all too seriously, it should be FUN for you and the children!

I truly hope this little guide has been helpful and encouraging for you budding puppeteers and wish you all the best on your puppeteering journey. It's a journey well worth taking!

Printed in Great Britain
by Amazon

20887195R00031